BERLIN

PORTRAIT OF A CITY

BERLIN

PORTRAIT OF A CITY

Photographs by
STÉPHANE DUROY

Introduction by *DAVID AIKMAN*

A BULFINCH PRESS BOOK LITTLE, BROWN AND COMPANY

BOSTON TORONTO LONDON

First United States Edition
First published in France as *Berlin, Ville Ouverte* by Éditions Nathan

ISBN 0-8212-1827-1
Library of Congress Catalog Card Number 90-55-458
Library of Congress Cataloging-in-Publication information is available.

Bulfinch Press is an imprint and trademark of Little, Brown and Com-
pany (Inc.)
Published simultaneously in Canada by Little, Brown & Company
(Canada) Limited

PRINTED IN FRANCE

BERLIN: A CITY FOR ALL EPOCHS

by David Aikman

Ever since it was first granted a city charter by the margrave (ruler) of Brandenburg In 1237 on the banks of the River Spree, Berlin has tantalized, challenged, and seduced both its foes and its rulers. Its geographic position has always been envied: well within reach of the great metropolises of Western Europe, but on the cusp of the East as well; Berlin is only forty miles from the Polish border. Even today, East Berlin's international airport of Schönefeld is host to dozens of daily flights to and from Moscow, Prague, Warsaw, Budapest, and Sofia, as close in flying hours as are Paris and London from West Berlin's Tegel Airport. European business planners have long daydreamed about the latent geographical advantages of Berlin — if the city were ever to gain full access to the outside world.

For forty-four years after World War II, that "ever" seemed as remote to West Berliners as the possibility of flying to Mars. For eleven months from June 1948, their half of the city, occupied by the Americans, British, and French, was cut off by land from the rest of Europe by a Soviet army blockade. That the city survived at all was due to the heroic airlift by Allied pilots. Then, from August 1961 onward, the Wall dominated the landscape, twenty-eight and a half miles of ugly concrete and barbed wire, separating, seemingly for all time, East and West Berlin. A further hundred miles of border fortifications surrounded the rest of the western half of the city, sanitizing the rural hinterland of East Germany from the contagion of capitalist urban glamour. About five thousand brave men and women managed to penetrate these fortifications in their quest for freedom, but at least seventy-nine died in the attempt.

Curiously enough, that "anti-Fascist protection wall," as East German leader Walter Ulbricht characterized Berlin's most famous post–World War II architectural creation, was not Berlin's first wall. When the city was far smaller, Frederick William I, appropriately nicknamed the Drill Sergeant, constructed a barrier around the city during 1713 and 1714 to prevent Berliners from evading military service in the Prussian army. That Berlin tradition of resistance to authoritarian rule has been a noble impulse for more than three hundred years, through surges of nationalist fervor and foreign conquests and occupations.

The tradition has a cultural origin that continues to give Berlin its great cosmopolitan personality. Despite a reputation as the lair of German nationalism, Berlin in fact offered refuge several times to foreigners fleeing political oppression. Persecuted French Huguenots constituted the first great wave of politically motivated immigration, in the 1680s and 1690s. The immigrants were educated, skilled, and multicultural. They instinctively rejected Prussianism, that peculiar obsession with discipline and order, and thus helped shape a vital aspect of the city's abiding character, a witty and mocking attitude toward state pomposity that was later to madden kaiser and führer alike.

Further influxes of French, Flemish, Bohemians, and Swiss in the 1740s and 1750s under Frederick the Great helped transform Berlin into one of the most elegant and cultured cities in Europe, the "Athens on the Spree," as nineteenth-century admirers dubbed it. The glorious Brandenburg Gate was erected to commemorate the Treaty of Basel between Prussia and France in 1795. When Napoléon occupied the city in 1806, he ordered the famous statue of the Goddess of Victory, with its chariot and four horses, the Quadriga, to be sent back to Paris. The chariot and its horses did not return until 1814, on Napoléon's first European defeat and exile. By then, the famous University was established in the city. Karl Marx studied here in the late 1830s, and he and Engels caroused irreverently with radical followers of the philosopher Hegel. After the failure of radical revolution on the Continent in 1848, Marx and Engels took socialism into exile in England. German intellectualism, meanwhile, turned conservative and nationalistic. When the Prussian statesman Otto von Bismarck proclaimed the German Empire in Berlin in 1871, the University of Berlin was already deeply influenced by the dark philosophical strains later to emerge in Nietzsche and the obscurantist ramblings of Nazism.

Physically, though, Berlin by then was already a handsome, open, ambitiously designed city that inexorably drew more and more Germans from the provinces. By 1900 the population had nearly tripled, to two million from 700,000, and by 1920 that figure had doubled again, to four million. The great landmarks of the center of the imperial capital were by now world-famous: the stately avenue Unter den Linden, the Reichstag Building, the Royal Opera House (now East Germany's State Opera), the University. A late nineteenth-century Baedeker described Berlin as "the greatest purely modern city in Europe." American visitor Mark Twain had a similar judgment. "It is a new city," he said, "the newest I have ever seen . . . and it is not merely in parts, but uniformly beautiful."

That beauty was later to be pounded into rubble by 360 American and British bombing raids and a Götterdämmerung artillery bombardment by 22,000 Soviet guns in the last few weeks of World War II. Ten square miles of the city was almost completely leveled, including several of its most gorgeous buildings. Yet the physical devastation only followed the twelve years of spiritual desolation of Nazi rule, which was itself a sort of revenge for the earlier triumph of the city's cosmopolitan tendencies. Like antagonistic spirits wrestling for the city's soul, in fact, nationalism and cosmopolitanism seemed to be at permanent war with each other once Berlin emerged as a fully fledged national capital on the world stage in the last quarter of the nineteenth century.

The total and brutal triumph of this nationalistic spirit could not have seemed possible in the 1920s to the leading lights of Berlin's astonishingly rich, risqué, and cheeky culture. The *Goldene Zwanziger* (Golden Twenties) had erupted. Kurt Weill, Arnold Schönberg, and Bertolt Brecht were just three of the world-famous names in theater and music whose brilliance and creativity became synonymous with the city itself. Another prominent resident for a while: Albert Einstein.

But the creativity of the twenties had a wild and bacchantic side, fostered by the grim memories of World War I and the humiliation of Germany's defeat and international reprimand at Versailles in 1919. It was a time of rapid fortunes, callous consumption, and decadence. In many ways, Berlin's cosmopolitanism of the 1920s was a final fling of irresponsibility before Prussian self-discipline reimposed itself on the nation. Topless dancing and singing—the American Josephine Baker at the piano—transvestism and other radical practices flourished there with impunity as they did nowhere else in Europe or America. The climate reflected a genuine cultural tolerance and openness in the very heart of Prussia.

Presciently, Goethe himself had written of Berlin during the reign of Frederick the Great: "To keep above water in Berlin one has to be somewhat coarse oneself."

Berlin's mixture of rough licentiousness and more polished iconoclastic wit has survived remarkably well to the present time. During the Nazi period, the tradition went instantly underground but reemerged after World War II, seemingly as vigorous as ever. The Huguenots might not be amused at the current form Berlin's tolerance of the grotesque has taken, but today's permissiveness — like that of the 1920s — has its roots in the heterodox ideas and customs imported to Berlin by these refugees from France. Unfortunately, not all of Berlin's recent immigrants have flourished as well as the early French settlers did. After two decades of uneasy residence as *gastarbeiter* (guest-workers), Berlin's Turkish population of some 100,000 still remains largely unassimilated into Berlin society.

The city's daring entertainment is best characterized by that great institution, the *kneipe,* or nightclub. Witty satire has always been a signature element of its entertainment. *Kneipes* were back in business, at least in the western half of the city, not long after World War II, helping to restore to the war-ravaged city its sense of irreverence and fun. In recent decades, the wittiest *kneipen* have been located in East Berlin. The bite of satire, after all, is usually sharpest where the pain of oppressive politics is the severest. But since the breakdown of the Wall, even East Germany's sardonic humorists have begun to grumble that their material is crumbling before their eyes. The fat and slow-moving target of satirists, the East German politburo and its attendant bureaucracy, has sunk irretrievably into the swamp of Communist collapse in Eastern Europe.

Berlin's humor, doubtless, will find spicy new targets, perhaps as East and West Germans alike take a harder look at themselves and their former capital city in the wake of reunification. As for Berlin itself, when united, it is likely to be contrarily both less and more than the sum of its two halves. Less, because no German government is likely to subsidize the colossal cultural duplication that flourished in West and East as capitalism went toe-to-toe with Communism in the late twentieth century. To offer some examples: there are two international-class opera companies, the Deutsche Oper in West Berlin and the Komische Oper in the East. There are two museums of Islam, two museums of Egyptology and two of East Asian art. West Berlin's Dahlem Museum contains the bust of Nefertiti; East Berlin's Pergamom Museum houses the Pergamom Altar and a reconstruction of the city gates of Babylon. As for the forty drawings by Botticelli, half are in the East and half in the West. Altogether, the governments of Bonn and of East Berlin have financed no fewer than twenty-nine state museums. Some of these, presumably, will be closed down as budgetary indigestion follows hard on the gluttonous celebrations of political reunification. And what of East Berlin's one and West Berlin's two major universities, sheltering 100,000 students in one city? Perhaps united Berlin will continue to finance them, but almost certainly without the profligate duplication of departments, programs, and research that has characterized two entirely separate academic establishments within the same city limits.

In many other respects, the new Berlin will be considerably more than the sum of its parts. Apart from anything else, it will be the capital of the largest and most powerful state in Europe, a newly self-confident dynamo of nearly eighty million inhabitants. The great centripetal forces of political reunification will draw into the city talent, trade, and people to a degree unimaginable when West Berlin was a gilded capitalist cage kept going at all only by generous handouts from the government in Bonn. There is already talk — enough to make the citizens of Frankfurt am Main wince — that the new Berlin will become Germany's financial capital once again. Even if that does not take place, a population explosion and a housing and commercial boom rivaling anything in the early twentieth century is likely to take place as the West German federal bureaucracy scrambles to invest the new capital with its presence.

A radical increase in population could mar the bucolic charms that made West Berlin so beautiful before reunification. More than a third of West Berlin's huge land area of 346 square miles is rural; some 25,000 acres are canals, lakes, and rivers. An astonishing fifteen and a half square miles of West Berlin are pure forest, in some areas so untouched that the city is the only one in the world where wild-boar hunting takes place. Windsurfing, waterskiing, iceboating, and nude sunbathing are just some of the activities West Berliners took for granted as a compensation for their city's beleaguered isolation from the thrusting growth and development of West Germany. As the population of a united Berlin soars, care must be taken that many of these pastoral and not so pastoral pleasures are not swallowed up by a new German megalopolis.

What will surely disappear, albeit gradually, are the quaint monuments of the city's half-century of quadripartite occupation. Checkpoint Charlie will probably survive, if only as a historical site, the figurative and literal guardhouse of Western civilization in the darkest days of the Cold War. Berliners will probably rather block out the reminders of those simultaneously menacing and comforting signs dotting the eastern edges of non-Communist Berlin: You Are Now Leaving the American Sector. Though they can be read as emblems of gratitude for Berlin's survival through the Stalinist siege, they could equally be interpreted as symbols of Germany's larger national humiliation beneath the boots of occupying armies.

For some time, of course, the fourteen thousand American, British, and French troops will maintain the institutional appearance of the Allied Kommandatura, the formal occupation authority that first took administrative power after World War II. The City Hall from which John F. Kennedy pronounced his immortal *"Ich bin ein Berliner"* speech in 1963 will surely still display its commemorative plaque. Something will have to be done to Tempelhof Airport, the old Luftwaffe base that is still the official military airfield of the American sector. But this and other municipal challenges left over from the time of Germany's division are likely to be dealt with swiftly once the momentum of Berlin's evolution into Germany's re-newed capital takes hold.

We can mourn, briefly, the eccentric, exciting Berlin that was the frontier post of the West during the darkest Cold War epoch. The richness of the espionage lore of Le Carré and Ludlum, the sense of fear and uncertainty that accompanied every American on his or her first visit to East Berlin, the gloomy, deserted East Berlin U-Bahn stations as the commuters from the West roared through, the sense of delight in watching the sun form a cross on East Berlin's gigantic 1,197-foot television tower — "the Pope's revenge," the irrepressible West Ber-liners called it: all these are memories and experiences woven into the fabric of Berlin as richly as the contributions of the early Huguenots. We will miss them.

But we will watch with fascination and not a little uncertainty as the new Berlin rises up amid a united Germany. Nationalism has adorned Berlin architecturally in the past, just as it has ravaged it morally. It may be that the energies un-leashed by *wiedervereinigung* (reunification) will usher Berlin into a new heyday in which pride in Germanness avoids arrogance and where four decades of democracy prepare Germans to welcome barbed, irreverent wit rather than to smother it. Perhaps no city in the world is better prepared philosophically to cope with its reemergence as a capital without losing its head. Somehow, the city has always outlived its disasters, outwitted its conquerors, and outjoked the governments that ruled it.

SIGNIFICANT DATES IN BERLIN'S HISTORY

1237 Berlin is founded on the banks of the River Spree.

1415 Frederick von Hohenzollern, a south German nobleman, is granted the title "Elector of Brandenburg."

1486 The city becomes capital of the Brandenburg state.

1539 As the Reformation engulfs Germany, Brandenburg becomes one of the "protesting" states.

1618–1648 As the Thirty Years' War between Catholics and Protestants rages across Europe, Berlin is devastated.

1685 Thousands of French Huguenots settle in Berlin after their expulsion from France.

1701 Prussia and Brandenburg join together to become the Kingdom of Prussia.

1713 1714 Frederick William I, the "Drill Sergeant," erects a wall around Berlin to keep its discontented citizens in.

1740–1786 Frederick the Great encourages a second wave of massive immigration into Prussia and Berlin.

1791 Completion of the Brandenburg Gate.

1806 Napoléon occupies Berlin.

1848 After abortive revolution in Berlin, Prussian troops return and establish martial law.

1871 German Empire proclaimed and King William I is crowned kaiser (Caesar).

1933 Hitler is named chancellor. Fire in the Reichstag.

1936 The Olympic Games open in Berlin.

1938 Anti-Jewish pogroms take place throughout Germany during and after "Kristallnacht."

1945 The Russians, Americans, British, and French conquer Germany and divide Berlin into four zones of occupation.

1953 East German workers' revolt crushed by Soviet tanks.

1961 The Berlin Wall is erected in August.

1963 President Kennedy makes his Berlin speech.

1970 The beginning of East-West German dialogue when West Germany's chancellor, Willy Brandt, meets East German leader Willi Stoph.

1972 Quadripartite agreement on Berlin between four occupying powers.

1978 Erich Honecker becomes East German leader.

1982 Helmut Kohl becomes West German chancellor.

1987 President Reagan visits Berlin and challenges Mikhail Gorbachev to abolish the Berlin Wall.

1989 May 2. Hungary cuts its barbed wire "iron curtain" with Austria.

August. A total of 20,000 East Germans flee west via Hungary and Czechoslovakia.

September 28. First major demonstration in Leipzig.

October 1. First "freedom trains" arrive in West Germany from Prague and Warsaw with 8,000 East Germans.

October 6. In East Berlin for the fortieth anniversary of the German Democratic Republic, Mikhail Gorbachev urges German youth to be patient.

October 18. On alleged grounds of ill health, Erich Honecker resigns all his Party and government positions.

November 10. Hundreds of thousands of East Germans cross the Wall to the West for their first visit in three decades. East Germany announces "free and secret-ballot elections."

November 13. Hans Modrow becomes head of the East German government; 5,188,510 visas for the West are issued by East German authorities from a total population of 16.7 million.

November 28. Helmut Kohl presents to the Bundestag, West Germany's parliament, his reunification plan.

December 17. The East German Communist Party, formally known as the Socialist Unity Party, changes its name to the Party of Democratic Socialism. The Staatsicherheitsdienst, or Stasi, East Germany's secret police, is dissolved.

December 21 and 22. In the presence of Kohl and Modrow, the Brandenburg Gate is opened.

1990 February 8. Modrow acknowledges the collective responsibility of the German people and "its remorse for the terrible crimes committed against the Jewish people."

March 18. In the first free elections in East Germany in four decades, a conservative alliance led by the Christian Democrats wins 164 seats, the largest block, in the parliament.

April. Lothar de Maizière becomes non-Communist prime minister of the German Democratic Republic and sets plans to merge East Germany with the West.

2

6

8

10

12

13

14

15

18

22

28

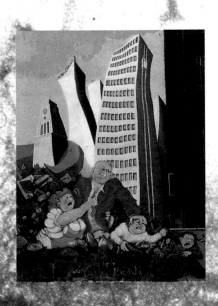

57

59

61

62

66

71

Macht Berlin zu einem Symbol
für ein neues politisches und menschliches Denken
_____us und Sozialismus
_____oika

75

LIST OF PLATES

Acknowledgments

Christian CAUJOLLE, Director of VU agency
Wolfgang BEHNKEN, Artistic Director of *Stern*
Marcel LEFRANC and Zina ROUABAH of VU agency
Tala SKARI
Loïc DUROY
Rémi BERLI
I especially thank the Ministry of Foreign Affairs (Secretary of State for International Cultural Relations) for the Leonardo da Vinci grant.

These photos were taken with LEICA equipment, M cases, and Summicron and Elmarit lenses.

The collected photographic work of Stéphane DUROY is represented by VU agency.